A Little Book of Blooms

Lizzy Polishan

D1293704

Portals to the Divine & LP Poetry

First Edition

2020

ISBN: 978-1-7360018-0-6

www.lizzypolishan.com

Table of Contents

enjoy.

hoya
carnosa

Hoya Carnosa

Before we were flesh-wrapped and body
before we were voice

we were
a spark

in a silent dark place
that was

before sparks
before we
before place and dark and flesh.

It is possible
even now

to go back to that dark
silent place
that we came from

before *possible* even was.

dragon fruit tree

Dragon Fruit Tree

I am creative—I am the creator of
my own reality. I have control of
myself—my fate—my destiny.
Captain of my ship: I am
the boat and the waves. I am

the

sun

&

the

stars

the storm.

water
lilies

The universe already

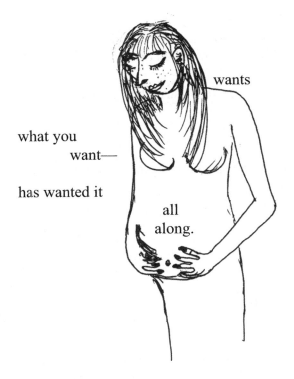

wants

what you
want—

has wanted it

all
along.

Water Lilies

Water lilies ache to be painted—
to show up as color on a brush and
be smeared into themselves on
green water, fixed,
                on fresh-stretched canvas.

*　*　*

God lives in the space between the water
lilies, standing there, aching to be and
the pink on the paintbrush in your hand.

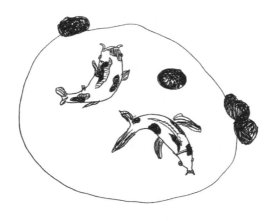

gerbera

Gerbera

My garden is my most beautiful masterpiece.
~Claude Monet

What is the point of art?
A Hopi Chief said we should

establish a routine to meet
the divine every day.

What makes art worthwhile?
When it is something worth

remembering or something delicious
enough to bring into being.

How do you know what to hold onto—
what's worth bringing to life?

.**

das meer leer

the truth isn't
something you can
shout into being but

something you can
feel when you're near its
silent presence as a

peaceful joy
singing in your heart

dahlias

I find myself
in that sort of loving where
I lose myself.

Dahlias

You find yourself terrified to become a mother because there is no more I, only we.

You find yourself comforted: *every we contains an I.*

You find yourself suddenly awake: *But where does that forgotten self go?*

You find yourself Googling dahlias.

You only need to dig up your tubers if you live somewhere where the winter gets too cold.

You find yourself in the minivan. You find your way to the nursery. You find yourself choosing red.

You find yourself at the cash register carrying more than you can afford.

You find yourself unloading armfuls of tubers from your trunk, bringing them out to the back-yard.

You find yourself in the digging—the making of the holes.

You find yourself hungry.

You find yourself hot.

You find yourself going inside.

You find yourself in English as a subject or object—like—I to me, him to he, her to she.

You find yourself in the pushing of boulders, forever, up the hill.

You find yourself in the stillness before the rock rolls down.

You find yourself abandoning Sisyphus before you reach the end of the myth.

(You find yourself with a watering can.) (You find yourself kneeling in the dirt.)

You find yourself writing.

Writing lets you figure yourself out, before you go off talking to the world.

You specifically remember being a koi fish one time—or at least, you remember the dream.

How many dreams have you forgotten?

How many dreams have you:
> a) forgotten you've forgotten
> b) forgotten to remember
> c) forgotten before you woke up??

How many dreams have you written down?

You find yourself writing down your dreams.

You find yourself with fishscales under your fingernails, drinking some water from the sink.

We are all koi fish, in the koi fish water. We are not going extinct.

You find yourself in the silence before you ink the next line.

You specifically remember being a poet one time.

You find yourself with a watering can. (You find yourself kneeling in the dirt.)

What is it about these "disruptions to momentum" that make pendulums and plums feel the same?

You find yourself writing a poem.

Poetry gives you the space to be free, and in this freeing, a place to let your self grow.

(You find yourself moving a rock. You find yourself hot in the sun.)

You find yourself thinking that deadheading sounds dirty, a lot dirtier than it actually is.

You find yourself sharing your dream journal with someone who sort of studied Freud.

You find yourself "reframing": they're *poems*, I think.

You find yourself huge. You find yourself in the kitchen. The kitchen is never closed.

((You find yourself in a writing group. Please avoid clichés.))

You find yourself doing the work. You find yourself grateful for the work.

The work means we're together. The work means you've arrived.

You find yourself writing something—any-thing—by the mountain of dirty dishes.

anything.

I need to keep writing to keep track of myself.

(You find yourself remembering more and more—remembering to do less and less.)

The effort to remember is immense.

In memory we become whole—in remembering we become anything at all.

You find yourself writing more reminders than poems or dreams these days.

You find yourself in the kitchen.

The kitchen is never closed.

You find yourself fingering figures on the win-dows in the frost.

Winter is Coming.

You find yourself quoting tv shows you can't re-member watching or even whether you watched them or not.

You find yourself in the garden again.

You find yourself on your knees.

You find yourself in the digging—in the making of the holes.

You find yourself in the garage, putting your tubers upside-down to drain.

You find yourself forgetting three times to turn your tubers right-side up.

You find yourself suddenly awake.

It is worse to lose the tubers or the memory of the blooms?

Have I forgotten more memories or unremembered things?

You find yourself remembering you've forgotten to write down your dreams.

(You find yourself forgetting to write a poem.)

You find yourself standing in the garage.

You find yourself looking for your tubers.

You find yourself forgetting where they went.

A memory is power because it lets you hold onto something instead of something else—

and—it doesn't let THEM forget.

You find yourself looking for paper and a pen.

It's not that we remember what we lost—we remember there's nothing to find...We always already are—

w h o l e.

You find yourself with a Post-It and a crayon.

You find yourself *writing.*

You find yourself forgetting what you wanted to say.

24

Portals to the Divine

There are no good
days or bad days—

just

days

where, when confronted with
the Divine,

you reached out to touch her

or not.

pink
orchid

Because I
am nothing,
I can be

a
n
y   g.
t   n
h i

.

Pink Orchid

Whisper her into existence,
hold the breath of her name in your heart.

We spiral tighter—
brighter—in the darkness,
circle the spark.

Climb inside this twilight
flower, holding herself closed
tight—let's stay here together

     Suspended

until

     she breathes open, into the night.

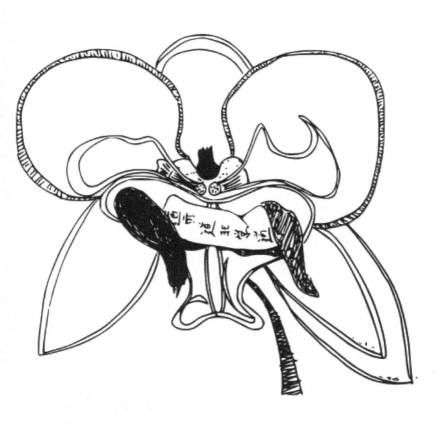

flower
matango

God speaks through me
when I let Her.

*How could I ever worry about
what to say?*

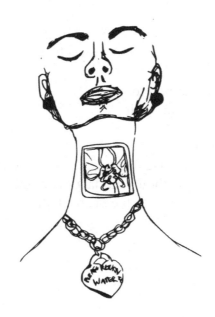

Flower Matango

I am the   e n t i r e
u n i v e r s e   and everything
about me   is small.

All
of
my
power,
most
truly
myself,

has nothing to
do with   me—

it comes   from the
Universe that beats within me and
without, and laces my heart
to the heart of all

things. (P   u   l   l   the

                    r
                     e
                    d

                    s
                         t   r
                              i   n

                                        g
                                          s.
)

                                        When
                                        y o u
                                        weave

                    together
                enough uncuttable
        thread, you'll make an invisible

                    blanket. Under the
                    cover   of nothing,
                    we'll l e a d each
                    other finally h o m e.

lipstick plant

Lipstick Plant

Sparks a match, my whip-quick aunt,
drops the dead wood in cold dark.
Wishes whispered, lipstick plant
hears: ignites her heart gold—sparks.

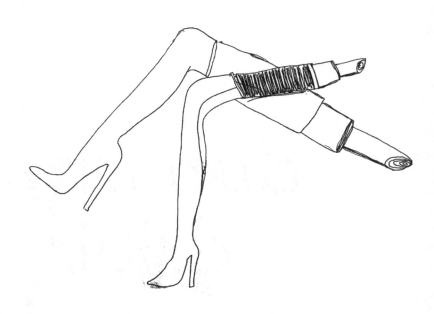

dahlias,
dried,
revisited

I'm not choosing you
because
you're all I've got—

I'm choosing you because
you're all I want.

Dahlias, Dried, Revisited

Jesus is the spooky
dried dahlia bouquet
Pinned on a board on
my MacBook screen.

On your Galaxy,
you're Googling
brewed witchy
punch and how to
peel grapes *fast.*

In this billow-white shift
I'm not sure who
I'm supposed to be, but
you say I look like Wendy,
that chick from Peter Pan.

I gave you the fish eye and
you let me have the cheek
even though I ate the other one
already. When Trick or Treat

shows up on our porch
you'll pass out candy to
a mummy and a fairy/queen and
the tiniest pumpkin twins
I've ever seen, and

you won't notice but—
I'll let the littlest ghost
feel my full moon
belly and whisper to her

wide eyes—*Yes, it's real.*

fairy
succulent

What I have is
what I would have

chosen

given the choice of
anything in the world.

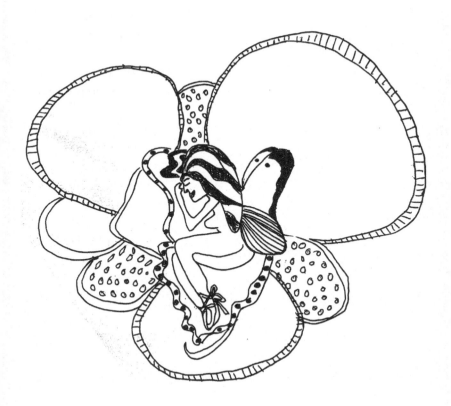

Fairy Succulent

i find myself in love—
when the self i constructed

when the girl i think i am
slips away and

for a moment
everything focuses on

something dancing
outside me,

something i feel dancing
deep within—

in loving that,
I is lost—

in that loving
i am found

[the snow is melting]

And it's all the worst of the I—
       the lies and ego and slant—
that melts away quick as
       snow into an open flame

    in love.

tradescantia
zebrina

Tradescantia Zebrina

A
Black train—
a bejeweled tunnel—
when train clears the pass she'll
wander inside—along the tracks—to
see—what she thought were
jewels are faces—
smiling at
she.

A
Light
calls—soon
Darkness falls—she
sleeps on fettered tracks—they're
there, she knows—the faces—her comfort in
the black.

aloe
vera

Aloe Vera

Wear a red dress and meet me
in the Tiger Grove to dance—
we'll sway till sunshine yields
shadows on moss, lit by swaying lamps.

Quick blue shadows—my fingers play your spine—
eyes closed—foreheads pressed—all that's left is
swaying in fields of endless pink thyme.

*

Swaying in fields of endless pink thyme—
eyes closed—foreheads pressed—all that's left is
quick blue shadows. My fingers play your spine:

shadows on moss, lit by swaying lamps.
We'll sway till sunshine yields
in the Tiger Grove to dance—
Wear a red dress and meet me.

polka-dot
plant

When you stop thinking
about not having it and

you start to want it
because it brings you joy—

you'll realize

it's already

here.

Polka-Dot Plant

Skylark on her shoulder sings
the things she holds in her heart—
hearing my secret wants aloud, I
know we're not apart.

black lace
elderflower

We dug holes.

Dropped

seeds

in

dirt.

Then we weren't.

Eve Weaves through the Fish-Shaped Leaves

The way you take my hand &
lead me to the garden to
smell the lemony blooms is
nothing like the way
you shyly nudged my elbow
the day we planted everything—

Black Lace Elderflower

We don't have a choice:
we are not the people who
dropped the seeds in the dirt,
    by the time we come to see

the blooms—but who knows
if you will be the one to take up
my hand and lead me to the
    garden, or if you will stand by

the lamp alone and watch him
    carry me away.

(*)

Whenever you choose   something,
a billion things that   could have been
              die—

        whenever you choose
something,   a billion possibilities
        are born.

peony

Stringing, Together

Let us make our way through the low
valleys of the humble little virtues. There
we will see roses among the thorns.
                    ~St. Francis de Sales

To choose some thing
freely
over literally billions of other
possible things—if
that's not love, I don't know what is.

To let yourself
be chosen
freely
by the same person
you chose to love over
billions of others—
I can't think of a more
joyful thing.

Peony

Love
is
choice plus
sacrifice.
I take you up and
let myself be taken by you.
We lay a billion other lovers to rest at our
wedding feast—*the first banquet of the magical*
  trillion we will with each other share.

Directions:
How to Come to Life

1. Find six sunwashed ocean-smoothed
stones & carry them—
everywhere—in your pockets.

2. Weave an ocean & an outfit
from rough seagrass, unwashed, &
wear it swimming.

3. Tread through your memories multiple times,
until the story is magical & halfway true,
& you've already walked through the places
you've always wanted to see.

4. Remember to take me twice a day
(with or without food).
By take me I mean
into your arms, in love.

5. Let yourself be taken
by me—in love, in my arms—too.

rex
begonia

In the beginning there was
nothing

and before that,

there
wasn't.

Rex Begonia

The Master said
he'd be here
sometime after dark.

Cool leaves—
rustle. One bramble
      falls
        at your feet.

Cool sweat—
        shiver. *Remember*

last time,
the pond burned red?

Cool moss—
springing—
Your soles wring
        the Earth.

Cool silver—
pond's edge: *a
silkworm—or—
a silken seam.*

***

Cool moonlight
changes,
cupped in your palms—

through your fingers

black water

slips

away.

air
plant

Air Plant

When the young yogi
told the master how
he wanted, more than
anything, to go to the
Himalayas, for that
would be where he could
find his peace, the master
said: Do you have a quiet
place in your home
where you can go, to
commune with the divine
each day?
The yogi said yes.
The master said
There is your Himalayas.

umbrella
plant

Umbrella Plant

We are all artists, clay and fishscales
under our fingernails,

lives malleable as a willow branch
stripped of its skin. Branches can be

bent into figures, you know. Figures can
take on human forms. When you're wine full and

sloshing you make the most sense: through
your nonsense divine words emerge.

When you scrape the peel off your life,
a delicate thing, the fruit inside *b r e a t h e s,*

and in the sunshine, quivers and dries.
When you pick up the dehydrated

thing it's become, you've got the only thing you'll
ever really have: Hard enough to hold forever or—

to throw—to shatter—to give yourself
the empty space to create something new.

canna
pretoria

Canna Pretoria

There are more things to do to
butterflies than catch them.

There are more things to do to
mountains than climb them.

There are more things to do to
caves than mine them.

There are more things to do to
beautiful things than buy them.

lucky
bamboo

There's nothing you
        ~~can~~ (have to)
do

                    to make me love you.

Lucky Bamboo

We are the music and the fossils,
the flute and the fern.

I am the loving and—
Don't look for me in a body.

I'm already inside of you.

1.

Our love is a hedgehog floating in a
plastic bucket: There's no reason for it and
there's no reason not to, and
there's nowhere to go. It's the smiling
that makes me smile.
There is no way to happiness but happiness
is the way.

2.

Our love is how we dug up the yard
in long strips and carried the dirt and
grass over our arms, swinging slow and
hanging deep, to your mother's yard
next door—together we laid our

grass on hers, interlocked the strips into
      a makeshift monochrome rainbow.
Later when we sit by your mother's fire,
      roasting sweet potatoes under the coals,
I will mandala-gaze at the grass and
      you will nuzzle against my shoulder until my
      body becomes the nest that we both call home.

      3.

      Our love is the line of bees
filing slow into the Shop Vac,
      hypnotic and calm,
one by one, against their will, but—
      Whose will is it, the filing of bees,
      slow and steady into the air that's
pulling them but not hard
enough to compel if they all decided
      enough is enough? They're only a
menace if they're angry and
      they're only angry if they're wet or
you hit them with a stick. They
writhe on the tree so it looks like
      it's alive—undulating—until the
      air takes them all one by one and—

one by one, they file into the
      dark plastic hose—
the uncrushed, collapsible spine.

But—
you wouldn't know the queen if
she stung you!

They're calmer than you think,
    bees,

    when they're wrapped around a tree,
    bringing dead branches to life.

+ + +

+ + +

We dance on bubble wrap—
Slow enough that every irregular
snap has the time to pop and
linger and die—

lives its entire life
alone under the flamingo clouds—
then—hits my heart—
e l e c t r i c.

*   *   *

Skies ripen nightblue—
under the star-hung heaventree,
my fingers read
the ancient grammar of your s p i n e

while
you handle my skin into a nocturne &
we alchemy the silence into something
we both can h e a r.

75

hyssop

Hyssop

Through time and love,
fused in mind,
all things will come and go—but

even love—time—and mind came first from *it*.

lotus

What isn't yours is
most truly
you.

Lotus

Poetry grows in the cracks of
        anywhere you let it.

Writing makes your life
something tangible
        enough to change.

Your mind lets you take up
the best of what is
and fuse it with the spark
        of what could be
        before it exists.

*   *   *

I take up the memories that
take me up to

        make up something like a self.

I take up the memories that
make me up to

        become something like a self.

I sift through my memories—
seashells in the sand—and
look for something like a self.

All I come up with
is an empty
conch in the mud,

until the wind blows and
the empty pink cave is
        speaking:

                and suddenly,
                I've got
                the whole ocean
                echoing
                from the nothing
                in my hand.

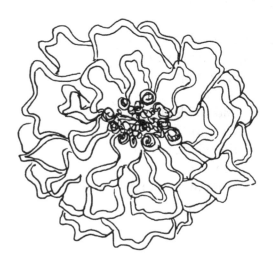

marigold

I am excited for all that IS and
all that's left to BE!

Marigold

Every poem is a fossil
of what had been
living inspiration—
messy cosmic union with
the divine.

(I have to compose
myself every day—
call myself into Being.)

A bird on the roof
of a small house
on the porch of
my big house—

by the time I write him
down and look up,
he's gone—
                  and I'm left
still
enraptured

by the click-scuff
          of his claws—

tulips

Tu

Where does the real mountain live—
in The Himalayas or in

the ants and the other small
things that live unnoticed in

your leg? Why did you ask

the question?

lips

Your Heart? When did my body become
     the gathering place for

the Earth? *What bit you
on its way up*

     to see me? *Why?* What
was that supposed to be—

    .

watermelon
sugar

Don't let a human
swallow you—

You will never
       see the sun—

You will live in a pulsing
cavern, darker than your shell,
pinker than the flesh
       you will never become.

Watermelon Light

You are a watermelon seed—
a hard dark thing
I'm scared to swallow,
scared it will grow
into
something

                    h u g e

inside me
without my will.

        * * *

I grow until it looks like I've
        swallowed a watermelon
whole—
        &—I love you the way a watermelon

        seed
loves a watermelon:

in the tiny dark seed,
the light of the watermelon l i v e s.

90

(*)

You carry the Himalayas in your heart.

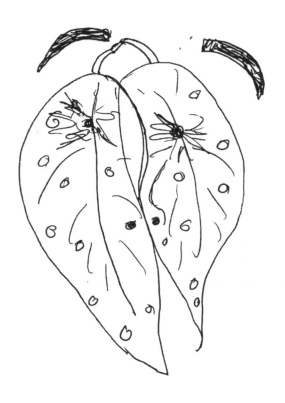

elephant's
ears

Elephant's Ears

Even when I show up
in that place
where nothing—
isn't—yet—

that darkness before
even nothing—

even then—I still
want *you.*

(*)

You're the thing I want to remember
    when everything else slips away.

(*)

Remember to
          r e m e m b e r.

japanese
chrysanthemum

This power within me—
most truly myself—
has nothing to do with me.

En Gedi

But nothing you work on is dull.
I am part of the beauty.

~Rumi

You, God, the giver of all
Dreams and lobsters. We should eat
soft pretzels in caves made
by monks—the pretzels,
I mean, not the caves.
I feel like a stone eroded by
the ocean and infused with
the salt. The dream is from you
for me and yet in me for you—
I'll share it with you, my
love. Is that the clever trick?
I too am an image—
maybe a dream—a woven
thing—woven by you.
(Please gather the straw
and braid it together
so it doesn't blow away.)
Weaver—dreammaker: and here
I am, a piece of the creation,
sharing myself and my lobsters
with the one who made us both.

Every time I whisper my
dreams in your ear, God gets to
know Himself for Himself.

Japanese Chrysanthemum

My daughter's dreams are
long and full of monsters and

sometimes she can fly.
She crawls into my bed and

whispers me her nonsense—
    the nonsense that is

e   v   e   r   y   t   h   i   n   g.

This Machine Kills Fascists

There is a sort of silence you can hear—

in between the notes of a song or
when you drive inside
a cool dark parking garage, out of the pouring rain.

old man's bones

Old Man's Bones

jacob's
ladder

You don't need to know how the ladder showed
up to take it up and climb
to what you want up there.

Jacob's Ladder

When you can look up
into the clouds and
through the clouds see
nothing, but know
what lives up there
already dwells in the
silence of your heart—
then
the ladder will appear—
praise every
blister—every rung—
every breath—every
inch of the joyful climb!

The climb is the work.
The work is love made visible.
The love is the link between
you and all you could be—
all you want and all
        you could ever have.

(*)

The ladder will bring you to where you want to go—to where you already are, in your heart.

old man's
bones ii

She doesn't know if she's sad
because she lost what they had or
what they could have been.

(*)

Join me under the soil—
first we'll smile then we'll
laugh till we both start to
glow as we realize
how we've never been apart.

(*)

Of course I believe in heaven—
if I have to look down at my body
literally decaying under the dirt,
I want to be at the sort of party
where it's literally impossible to run out of wine.

(*)

Your mother asked me if
I would ever leave you but
I thought she said *love you*
so of course I said

of course.

(*)

Wrap your roots around
my ribs until
I am part of the plane
         tree you've become.

Old Man's Bones II

You don't have a choice:
Your body became my shade.

But you are the tree I choose
to become—

when the time comes that
I can't choose anything
anymore.

Wrap your roots around my ribs &
drink my flesh into your leaves

until I am part of the plane tree
you've become—

until our flesh becomes again—
forever—*one*.

wheatgrass & lily

As soon as

we think
we know

NOTHING—

it
bec o m e s
       s o m e
    t h i n g
  &

    s
       l
       i
         p
          s
            a
              w
            a
          y

(*)

The vines that live in the
space between your ribs
link them together into
something almost beautiful,
something almost
          more than a cage.

(*)

I was amazed such words had come
out of my empty mouth.

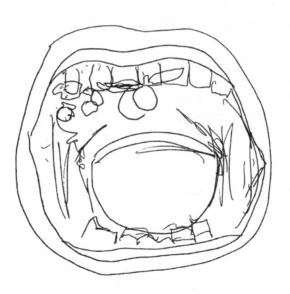

Wheatgrass I

1.

An orchard grows in your
stomach—
peaches and plums as
far as the eye can see—

yet you're walking around with
an empty plate asking
people for scraps of their stone fruits.

Why are you looking for
mangos in the grove when
infinite mangos live
already in your heart?

2.

Don't copy—steal.

3.

There is nothing to steal—
everything that matters
already lives within you.

Why put tracing paper over
fossils from the masters'
encounters with the divine &
try to pass off the product as
something even sort of magic
when the goddess who
beats in your heart aches to
dance in your hands and,
through your hands, be born?

Lily

I can paint you a lily in
a thousand different ways but if
you don't believe how
much I love you, what I give you will be
just a catalogue of images, full of
color and chaos, signifying nothing.

You always seem to want to transcend
something—to cast off the material as
meaningless and *climb*

somewhere better—

But when you show up in
your jeans, painstakingly
ripped for me,
I see fingerprints of your love—
in every hole, every bare thread—
every scrap of skin the space
between the strings reveals.

The point of the lily is not the lily and
 is not *not* the lily.

When I'm online shopping
I'm not really buying a romper but
I'm buying the way I want you
to look at me if we ever meet again—

It's not just that I want to
see you, or even you to see me—

I'm trying to show you—with
something white and flowy—
how I feel about you in the silence
between my words—*what the
silence between my words means.*

Lily II

It's not about *you*—but how the
space around you moves and
flutters and bends when
you walk in a room—
disruptor and shaper of nothing.

*　　　*　　　*

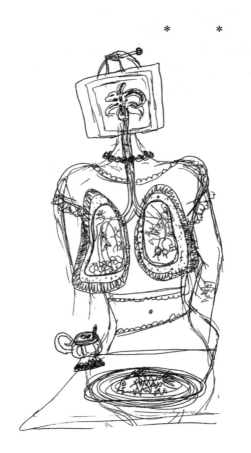

*　　　*　　　*

Praise be to God for the
NOTHING—for the air
outside you that defines
you—that makes it
possible for you to be
anything or anything else or
anything at all—the air

                    outside you that you can
                    take up and hold inside
                    your lungs before you turn

it back into breath, into the
air I will take up, move
through, disrupt—into the
nothing that defines me, too.

(*)

Everything without you was
within you first—

even now you can take up anything outside
you—
hold it in your mind—let it dwell again

within—

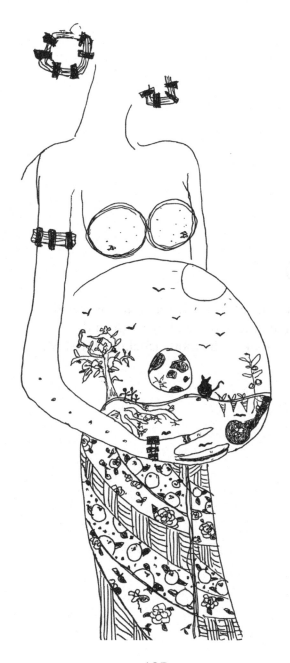

(*)

We are mostly air and water, fire-warmed,
non-metallic, sustained by earth, and—
　　　look at the motherfucking TREES!!

(*)

Even a subway ad
becomes a mandala
when you look
long enough to see
the weight of
the worlds it links together.

Even a paperclip
becomes ecstatic when
you hold it
long enough to feel
the weight of
the universe in its form.

* * *

THINGS FREEZE
　　　　the TIME that
they can't
　　　　unstick them
　　　　　　　　　　selves
from.

Wheatgrass II

The wheatgrass is the wheatgrass is the
water it drinks is the cloud the water
came from is the rain needling the river

brimming with the salmon that we ate for
dinner without any of the whisky that's still
waiting to be *aged* in dark barrels in the

basement that is—all of it—also
the wheatgrass. The wheatgrass
is the wheatgrass is the sunshine pulling

water from the rain-swollen stream is
the rain-swollen stream and the stream's
bank and the dirt of the bank that's the

same dirt keeping the wheatgrass grounded.
The wheatgrass is the wheatgrass is the shirt
pattern it will become and the

feet it will touch and the black of the cat
cat who nibbles at its tips. The wheatgrass is
the wheatgrass is the wheatgrass is not.

maidenhair fern

Your voice is something
less and more than body,
more and less than air—

more or less
the liminal space between
a lump of clay and God.

Maidenhair Fern

Power starts with a choice:
will we live as hostages to fear
or as hosts to the divine?

We are going to hurt so many people, intentionally or not,
simply by being incarnate and human and broken—but
power starts with a choice.

We will be hurt by so many people, intentionally or not,
simply by being incarnate and human and broken—in these
  encounters,
will we live as hostages to fear?

Unconnected, hate came quick and easy—
shots of whisky—
but will we live and die as humans broken
or as hosts to the divine?

(*)

You don't need
power over others
to be powerful.

roses

&

tree
stars

Not trees in fall unleaving
or springtime buds receiving
rain—not Joy & Sadness—
not imagination—not memory—
nothing that comes & goes—

What we want,
we already have:

the silent
presence behind all
s e a s o n s.

Tree Stars

Though Summer's over—
though it's October—

The moon always fills back up
              again.

          *   *   *

I can't crawl into your arms and
            hear that story anymore.

We can't watch that movie
      again.

The Land Before Time—isn't
                  —there.

              Now when you tell me I'm
braver than I believe and stronger than
I seem and smarter than I think,
you are speaking to a different person—
you don't exist anymore and
neither do I—but somehow
when you say that, the words cut
through time—*time falls away*—
and for a moment
we become what we had been—
we are lost and *we   are*   *found.*

138

The Shape of Bees

The tree was there before
the bees gathered around it like
a skin, pulsing—a cloth, dancing—
but would you say the tree is gone?
The tree was there before
and after the bees.

One day the tree will be gone too.

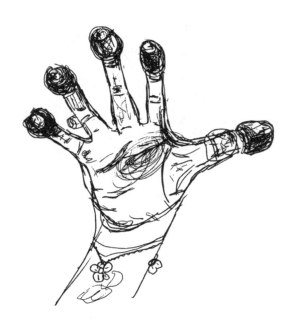

The Land Before Time

I found my grandma
watching kids' shows—
ancient creatures, animated,
lumbering around on the screen—

Why are you watching that?
I miss my kids.

Why don't you call them?
I can't.

Hofgarten

The tropical tree will stay green and
joyful forever—the tropical tree
will still die. We hold onto things
because we mistake them for the joyful
presence they came from. We hold
fast to riches because we mistake them for
the presence underneath, the silent
forever-abundance, from which they came.

(*)

You are and are not the flash of
quick hot union that made you possible—

that brought all the universe into being and,
in all the universe's things, still dwells. Any

one who looks at you can see the universe—
that you are and are not—in your cast,

the same way anyone who looks at you
can see your mother's ocean eyes

looking back, but know you are somehow—
different. Why do you think leaves have

matrix of veins under their plump skin,
and trees have a network of neurons under

the skull-dry earth? You are brothers,
you and the tree, your mind mirrored in his roots.

Within, without, one: you are and are not
      everything: the vine—the leaf—the fruit.

Tricolored (Double Knockout, Rambling) Roses

Wanting anything, what you crave is this
thing you lost or that thing you never had.
The source—of all things you can have or miss—

keeps you up late, searching how to attract joy
and avoid pain. You've stopped—it makes you too sad—
wanting anything. What you crave is this

day lived again so your restless nomad
soul won't need to—later—mourn her still-living un-little boy.
The source of all things you can have or miss

must be playing games, because you miss lily pads
on ponds that no longer exist. So enjoy
wanting anything! What you crave is this

thing you can't have. But—what comes and goes, fad—
not it. Grief and joy—not it. To employ
the source (of all things you can have or miss)

to fulfill your will—not it. It won't come coy—
it won't leave. (&—you don't really want the lilies or the
schoolchild plaid)—
Wanting anything, what you crave is this:
the source of all things you can have or miss.

145

china doll plant

How do you sort between the
suitors and what's real
when God lives in every lily?

China Doll Plant

Fertilize your houseplants with fishbones—
the malt wine goes to the horses outside.

The best things grow when you're drunk
on something and looking at the full moon.

(I thought I'd wrap you up in cellophane &
keep you in my kitchen but the
houseplants don't need any more shadows—
don't like anything waiting around to be
opened or to be set free.)

Our gardens grow in Tuperwares and
the earth under your fingernails
glitters in sunlight: moonbeams
caught in midnight waves, between the
bluegills and the swordfish, the starfish and the gods.

We live in the space between
the shoreline and the orchids,
where light exists only as
slant and silver sparkle in the sand.

Sometimes when we're looking at something &
drunk on the moon, we'll bend
together (horses in love) and water
each other (with malt wine and whisky)
until our bodies can (almost) forget

the difference between a Garden and Flesh.

sunflower

I am so grateful that I am exhausted from
the work of loving you and
not from the bleary-eyed insomnia of missing you.

Sunflower (Please Return to Water)

I wear myself out and struggle with the sun.
And what a sun here! It would be necessary
to paint with gold and gemstones.

~*Claude Monet*

I am exhausted—the sort of
exhausted that makes your
eyelids ache with the weight of
trying to defy gravity and
your body ache with the burden of
trying to defy itself a little
longer. It's the sort of
exhausted you feel in your bones.
Some people are more exhausted
than me, and I wish them relief, and
I am still exhausted, and
some people are less exhausted
than me, and I wish them rest, but
I am still exhausted.
But love is the sort of thing that
feels exhausting sometimes—
and all the extra washing and cooking

means you are here and
we are still together!

I'm exhausted means
I'm still the one you lean on.

And you're exhausted, too.

        ***

We take turns staying up
with the lamp—

until all
the kerosene has drunk itself gone and
        the light burns out, and rises.

(*)

*Any way, I'm going to be
exhausted—in staying up all
night missing you or in
staying up all night with you or in
staying up all night keeping watch
so you can sleep in peace,
    if just for one n i g h t.*

(*)

Praise be to the exhaustion—
it means you're awake!

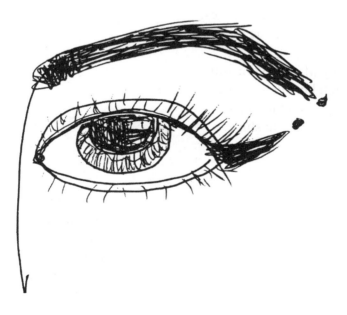

Sunflower

I asked what you wanted &
you said summer and
   I said *I'll get a tattoo.*

They studded my hips with roses,
bunched & scattered—
   ruby constellations.

They covered my back with
dahlias, black and silver—
every stage of their opening and closing
dancing across my spine:
a moon in all its phases,
   each one locked in t i m e.

They planted your sunflower
patch between each of my fingers—
   spread me apart
   for sunshine.

         *

        I've become
        nothing but
     all that you want &
       a universe
        frozen
       in time.

(*)

hold my hand and come to the window—
    it's starting to snow

white
roses

And even in the private universe of my dreams

I've

somehow

got

the idea

that

you love

me?!

White Roses I

Every night every one
simultaneously creates and dwells

in a private universe. This reality is most
purely myself: the only place where I am

a trinity—an artist, an artwork, a
viewer, at once. This most pure experience

of myself—and I'm not even awake to
see it! *And you will never see it at all.*

Still—where did you come from—in my dream?
Where did the garden where we meet—or

the flowers, heavy and sweet—or the
drop of your blood on the thorn of the rose

you're giving me—come from? And—where
did I ever get *the idea that you love me?*

In dreams we are

united—

not in
the world we experience

but

in our
experience of a   world

no one
else

will

ever

see.

White Roses II

The stars are beautiful tonight and
the lobster is sweet.
Every moment is a renewal.
You are something round and
wrapped
tight in gold foil.
Koi fish sing your name.
(Be melting snow—wash
yourself of yourself!)
Be a fire
fly!

(*)

Trees—living—grow
leaves. On trees—dead—
leaves grow.

Glory be to these two
types of trees and the
difference between them!

You too can be
a tree from which
life springs forth—or

one strangled up in
someone else's ivy.

pentas

Stop limiting your miracles
to the impossible —

every possible thing
incarnate is
the miracle and the proof.

(*)

Your name lives
silent
in the grooves of my soul.

This Machine Kills Fascists II

Our bodies are
electric
eclectic
power
machines.

Pewder
powder blue

power

machines.

Pink & toes & light—
organic

factory machines.

Pentas

We went into the scrap of woods
behind your clapboard house and
in a glass thing
in the dirt I found you.

*

I found you in a glass jar
half buried in the Earth
by the hole you said a basilisk made,
though we'd never see anything
slink in or out.

*

I forget to miss you when you're here.

When you show up at the
table where we shared so many
breakfasts, it's hard to
remember that you'll never eat
      here again. But
        every child dies, sooner or later.

＊

Who you are isn't who I
thought you'd be.
I think I like you
better than I thought.

I miss everything we
put in the glass jar and
everything we didn't.

＊

Even in a self stretching out
endless sunny day after sunny
day, then season after season,
the shoreline of an ancient
beach extending into
what seems like forever and yet—
even when life goes on like that
uninterrupted by death—

We're still laying to rest
what we were &
what we could have been
in a glass jar glinting in the dirt.

But there is such joy in
the way the sunlight glints on
the glass, and how
the sparks will dance

tomorrow—

as

—*the memory of the light.*

(*)

I'm mourning
everything that could have
been as much as
         everything that was.

(*)

Every dew drop on a blade of
grass is a miracle because
even if you're not into
dewdrops or grass or outside,
it's fucking amazing that
a world with dewdrops and
grass and outside even exists &
that you're around to see it!!

(*)

We are all
the universe
experiencing
herself.

hyacinth

Your body is proof that
God loves you and

is you.

Hyacinth

I don't want to take down the
poster of Kurt Cobain
taped to your wall because I don't
want to forget the you who
taped it up there or
the look in your eyes when you
did it—and—the way your cheeks
flushed peony, like the time you
came to me—breathless—
gathered—wildflowers!—sprouting
from your hand—and—their little
heads!—bowing—when—
          you gave them—away.

passion
flower

Forgive them, Father.

Passion Flower

Jesus loves the people
who put Him up
        &

the people who took Him
        down.

    Jesus loved Paul when Paul was Saul.

(*)

The light of the candles is One though
the candles are many—

are all candles, burning
eternal—in the same freaking love.

monstera & black poppies

Monstera

& even
faithful forever love

the kind that doesn't
crack
souls
but
sews them
together
will be
oblivion
or
suffering

depending on
who you are &
who

passes
out
first—
but you know
a love like that
lives
forever
somewhere outside the time that
let it be
anything   *at all*

Black Poppies

Does she fix her eyes
on the landscape,

     blurring by,

     or on the window—
     steady, still?

Does she fix her eyes
so she doesn't have to
watch his face,

or so
she doesn't
have to

imagine the way
his mother will lace
her fingers through his hair,
and, for the last time,
     whisper goodnight?

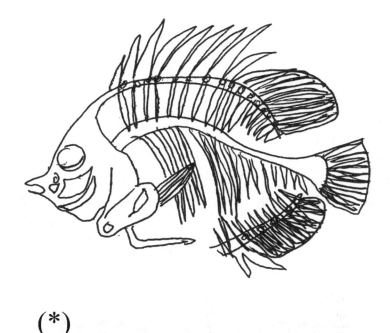

(*)

The Time that gives love the chance to unfold is the Time that spilts all lovers apart is the Time that will, eventually, weave us back Together.

fresh cut
dahlias

We are both

      something and empty

            space.

What matters is the

      emptiness.

Fresh Cut Dahlias

Capture a moonbeam's subtle blue—
How can you

form landscapes from petals and grapes?
Define the shape

of love with just an evening dress.
Of emptiness—

of everything laced with excess—
of dreams of mother's lost bracelet—
of all this, you're my favorite.
How can you define the shape of emptiness?

(*)

How can you hold nothing? or turn it into
ribbons—slice it, smooth as a butterstick left

out on the table all night?

(voidspace constellated)

Rain needles nothing into
ribbons, bunches, strange erratic

slices—then gathers itself into something,
a palm or a lake.
Some cosmic vase.

But when did rain become—
rain? Was rain rain before it had

a name? What came first—
vases or names?

The gathering—or the scattering—

(das meer leer)

You are the rain and I am the
          space between the drops—

                without you
I am nothing but

                without me

                              you
          don't
                    even

                    e

                         x

               i

                              S

          T

daffodil (narcissus)

LOOK AT ME.

.

I am POWER and grapefruit
and amazing

&

everything powerful
about me is
on loan from the divine.

Daffodil

You are the space
between the fleeting

shadows of this world
and the everlasting
         perfect of the next—

Let me hold you &
come to you—

       &—

Look at me!

I want to see
        the universe I look at
        all day

looking at me back.

(*)

You know:

What is isn't

                permanent—

this world of shadows and
appearances
is nothing
           compared to the
power from which it came—

        the power that still lives
        in your chest:
        a portable potable darkness
        you can swim in
                any time.

You know:

You find yourself when
     you   *let yourself*
f a l l   a w a y—

when you think about something
long enough that

only the thought
remains,
>*and* you *go to that space where*
>*your self*
>>*isn't*
>>>>*even a memory.*

You know:
even the thought falls away. Even
the power falls away.
Even you

can return
to that space before it all: the space that
>*will never emerge.*

(You know: I came into being
because of how obsessed
>>*with you I was.)*

Narcissus

How can I reach that loveliness
I see mirrored in the water?
~Narcissus

If I don't die
like Li Bai—
drunk and allegedly

bending over the side of a boat
trying to scoop up
handfuls of the moon like
it's not impossible—
what's the fucking point?

(*)

The divine, so personally invested in your wellbeing,
is literally obsessed with you—
you who is She—on loan and interest-free.

cloud nine
verbena

Cloud Nine Verbena

I love you
almost as much
as I love
the idea of what we could be.

carménère
grape vine

Carménère Grape Vine

Do you want some mangoes?
Close the door. We don't have any grapes?

                    You shift
                from one
            foot to
the other—

            your body is enough to
            blot out the whole sun.
                    No.
            Weather-changer goddess—

you stubborn,
                movable
                            mountain.
Yet—

            there is a smile
            you're hiding,
            in your settling in—

the flesh of the mango is sweet.

            Sweeter than I remember.

            Sweeter than grapes.

english
ivy

Memory and my arms are
the only places

you can take up and
          be taken up by, too.

English Ivy

Out past our ideas of right and wrong,
   in the field where the silent bird sings us together
      before any words have the chance to fail,

   I will pull your dark curl and
the spark it ignites in my chest, the boat that we came from,
      becomes the boat that we'll share to go Home.

   Undress my hands until the skin you find,
pied and ringed, sings you to insomnia,
             softly—a chorus of silver
      minnows, pleasant and cool. Only

      when your arms ring
the form of my bent body
      can we dreamers awaken and,
lucid in the darkness, call the Darkness we find *home*.

(*)

A memory can't love you back but
it can become, at any time,

the field where we first fell in love.

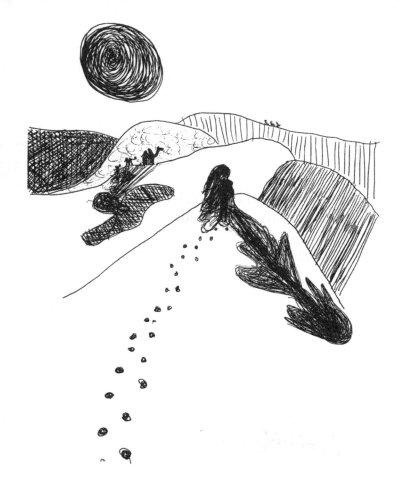

mojave—
pink

I don't trust you—

I am you.

I don't trust you anymore—
I've loved you so much
for so long—
I am you—you are—me

Mojave—Pink

Cross desert sands alone.
Every anonymous skull is a goblet.
The light is less than ash,
more than silver.
The nothing feels like the
desert, and the traveler feels like
navigating dunes on a starved
tiger's back. What is a tiger
when you can see his ribs?
Every rib cage echoes.
Sit with something until it
falls away—until you fall
away. Until you wake up with the
sun and let it carry you
somewhere you don't need
a night of dreams to stay awake.

that long
red
succulent
thing

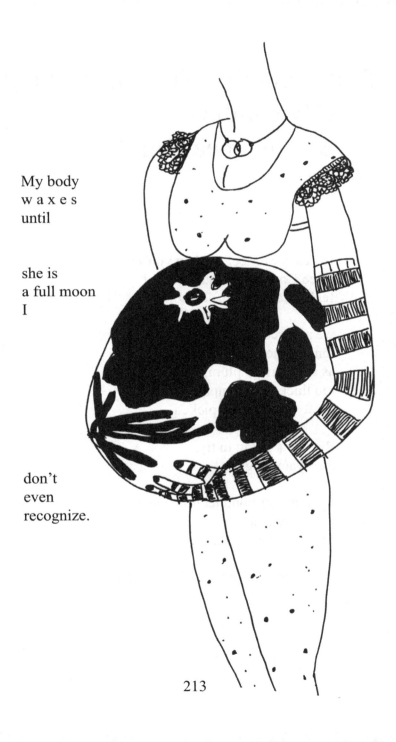

My body
w a x e s
until

she is
a full moon
I

don't
even
recognize.

213

That Long Red Succulent Thing (Hyacinth Girl & Chickpea King)

1.

It's easier to feel it when you're
three Coronas in and it sort of
feels like the truth. Tomorrow

we are free but
tonight the moon is heavy
as an overripe plum,
too thick with tempting
      juice to be picked.

But she's going to try,
the hyacinth girl—

she puts her bouquet down and
      reaches up
until her fingers skim the skin.

      She's going to give it to Him.

2.

The hyacinth girl sleeps on the rock.
The chickpea sprouts break ground.
Tomorrow, tomorrow—a rose petal,
        flaking off—
the moon shaves itself down.

> *What if I go crazy? What if I don't.*
> *What if I just grow and grow*
> *into who I really am—*
> *out loud, in front of—Him?*

When the moon is thinner than a fingernail,
she starts to go to Him.

3.

Follow me to the Pavilion.

We're looking somehow—down—
        at the lilypond—
and from this view everything is—
abstract and interlocking—
        Morse code, or something like that.

Like the Universe is whispering
        Wallala leialala or,
        everything
        I ever whispered, back.

4.

Darkness born from darkness.
The moon has closed his eye.
The empty in her arms is the empty in the sky.

Black night cicada lullaby.

She carries him the moon.
        She will cry.

        What are we but a string
        of moments
        laced together with silence?

Ghosts in the field, among the
                cabbage butterflies.

5.

Lay in the dark.
How are we still steady?
A darkness so heavy,
under its crushing—we   e x p a n d.

We are love and nothing, pressed together,
coming into being, under the weight of the night,
under and beside the moon.
                &.

The moon always fills back up again.

(*)

We are wine in dark barrels
waiting to be aged,
hoping old enough never comes.

The Silver Cord, Severed

I am afraid to be BIG because
I am afraid to be SMALL after
my body has swollen.

I'm afraid
THE SMALL I WAS BEFORE
won't feel the same
after I've been BIG.

But she's all about
AGAIN, the divine.

Besides,
so much is
tropical.

(The moon always fills back
up again).

The Wheel by the Well

You are not
the divinity
dwelling in your chest.

Even your dreams are
on loan from the gods.

> Yet—

every dream
sparked in you
        first.

&—

What are you
other than someone's God—

or: the Universe experiencing
        Herself?

burro's tail &

creeping jenny

3:18

When you want to be a tree,
you've arrived.

Creeping Jenny /

I want to get to that
breathless place where

I don't even love you
anymore

because
there is no more
you to love or
I to do the loving—
and we are
simply
one—

even if it's just for
one
clumsy moment
t/fumbling
in the sort of dark

where even matches
can't strike

/ Burro's Tail

I want
the sort of love where—
      for one breathless moment—
you don't even love me anymore
because
you and *I* drops away and
we are just one,
      fumbling in the dark—

but what I want even more than that is
      the sort of love where
we've been together for so long that
      I don't even love you anymore
      because
      I and *you* drops away

even when we step into the l i g h t

(*)

when grapes turn into wine or
bees build honeycombs—
they are wanting this divine—
love—

the memory of it
stitched into the fabric of their being
so much so that they don't even
need to think about it
to know that's exactly what they are

zig-zag cactus

//

white flower

Zig-Zag Cactus

Night will ask
Day to come
She will reach out and
They will never be one

Vagabond Lovesong

It's hard to wind down
after the NIGHT—
bleary-eyed, with all your
dreams in the paper-bag
between your knees—
when you look up at
the subway car window—
        who do you see??

        ***

Glory be to God for Seattle—
for Space Needle and fresh air—
for clouds like freckles in
more than just a scrap of sky
and the daisies and the brews—
For brews in brown

paper bags
where there should have been dreams.

White Flower

*A white flower grows
in the quietness.*

*Let your tongue become
that flower.*

~ Rumi

1.

The baby bird died before
we could name him, so
we named him after he passed.

He showed up as fuzz in
a square of sunlight,
slanted through the slats. Something

in the naming made it a lot more sad.

2.

We can't talk about it so
we talk about the baby
bird, still in a square of slanted
sunlight—we give him
a name and make him a
crib from a matchbox and
say goodnight to the fuzz of him, instead.

3.

His mother goes on feeding everyone
else inside, while my
mother wraps him up and digs the hole.

4.

Somewhere some bird still croons
softly, something like a song.

hoya
carnosa ii

thank you

(*)

I've loved you so much
I have vanished—
only *loving* in the world remains

Hoya Carnosa II (2020)

Full moon on
July 4.

We light sparklers.

Everything smells
like sulfur. I'm so
obsessed with
sparks, yet when

actually confronted with
their incarnation

the most beautiful
part is the way
your face goes
golden in the glow.

      * * *

Mother stands on the
top step, draws a
circle with a sparkler, and
I catch a glimpse of how
she used to be—the
version of her that died
           before I arrived.

* * *

I'm exhausted from the
food and the ocean and
every so often something
electric bumping my leg.

* * *

On the second day I bought a Hoya—
when I returned to the nursery for the one
I photographed the day before,

    it was already gone.

(I hope it's somewhere lovely with
lots of sunlight, not too many
shadows, nothing wrapped and standing
still, waiting around to be free.)

* * *

I feel like this can go
on forever—I feel like
I'm not ready to
STOP. I feel like it's
the perfect time to
      get to the
           Holy End.

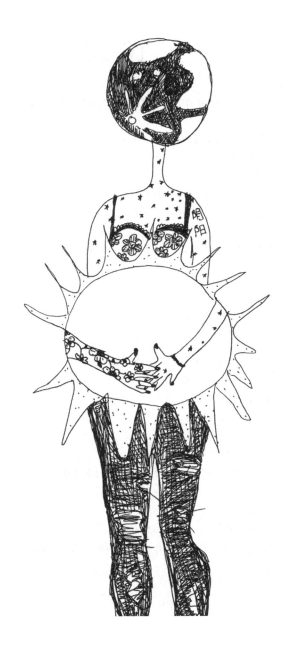

10:20

I am broken and I am angry and I love you.

There is nothing I can do to
make you love me
which means
there is nothing I have
to do. Thank you for the love.

*A silent voice comes to me in
the dark.*

In the hardest time, you
chose me—

Dear mom, my dear mom—
You gave up so much of
what you could be so I could
be anything at all.

Thank you. (I can never thank you enough)

Your body is the dark place
before my possible even was, the dark place that
said

yes.

(*)

You are
the dark place

before
possible
even was—and

yes—
you said *yes*—
I will—

yes

(*)

To: My Mom Lisa

Thank you for
literally everything.

THIS IS THE END

Made in the USA
Middletown, DE
27 October 2020